New Architecture in New Haven

The MIT Press   Cambridge, Massachusetts, and London, England

New Architecture in New Haven

Revised Edition

Don Metz

This book was set in Linotype Helvetica
by Atlantic Typographers
printed on Warren's Cameo Brilliant Dull
by The Meriden Gravure Company
and bound by The Colonial Press, Inc.
in the United States of America

Library of Congress Cataloging in Publication Data

Metz, Don.
  New architecture in New Haven.

1. Architecture — New Haven.
2. Architecture — Designs and plans. I. Title.
NA735.N39M4   1973   720'.9746'8   72-5839
ISBN 0-262-13095-5
        0-262-63045-1 (pbk)

The first edition of *New Architecture in New Haven* was published in 19
at the peak of the city's renewal, redevelopment, and building programs. T
late sixties marked the end of a decade of unprecedented architectu
activity fostered by energetic political leadership and an enlightened Unive
sity policy. Vast amounts of federal and state funds made possible the ne
highways, housing, schools, and industries that shaped the new New Have
Yale University's building program, led by its new residential colleges a
an expanded science campus, produced a record number of new buildin
and a master plan for future expansion.

This revised edition of *New Architecture in New Haven* brings the reco
to date and reflects, in its selection of projects, the change in the nature
architecture as it responds to the social and economic demands of the ea
1970's. Federal and state participation in the city's projects, as elsewhe
has dropped off significantly, and the University can no longer afford the r
of the extravagant architectural gesture. The resulting attitude seems to ha
diminished the quantity but not the quality of architectural expression. Inn
vative solutions in housing and structural systems have taken priority o
the elaborate spatial eloquence of the recent past. Included in this edition
a representative selection of New Haven architecture of the past fifteen yea

2

New Haven Common

In 1641, John Brockett developed a plan for the City of New Haven based on a symmetrical grid of nine squares. The central square was designated as the Public Common. Surrounding the Common today are various examples of the city's architectural heritage from the last three hundred years. These historic landmarks establish an attitude of scale and variety that is vital to the Common's function as a public park and meeting place in the midst of a busy city. Future projects around the Common must continue to recognize it as a constant point of reference in the changing profile of the city.

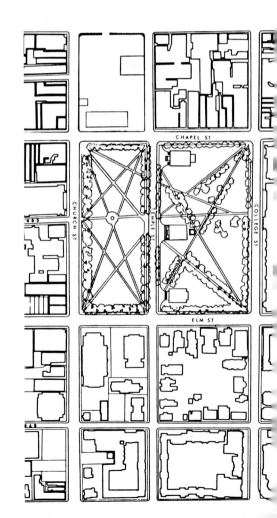

4

Yale Art Gallery
1111 Chapel Street

architect: Louis I. Kahn

The Yale Art Gallery
represents the first important
step in the University's
architectural renaissance
begun in the middle 1950's
under the late President
Alfred Whitney Griswold.
Smooth brick and glass
curtain walls sheath four floors
of open loft space. The
ceilings reveal an innovative,
tetrahedron-based structural
system that lends a rich
texture to the otherwise
simplified exhibition areas.
Sculpture courts on the north
side serve to integrate the
museum's interior with the
natural privacy of Weir Court.

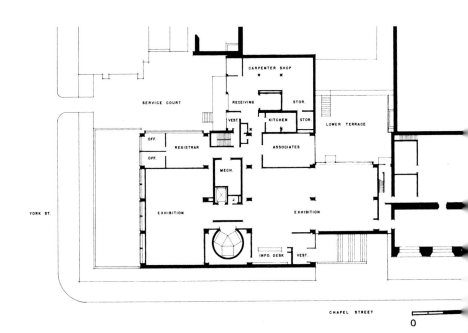

6

**Yale School of Art and
Architecture**
180 York Street

architect: Paul Rudolph

The Yale School of Art and
Architecture is occupied by
the graduate departments of
painting, city planning,
architecture, graphic design,
and sculpture. Organized
around four massive interior
columns, its nine stories are
broken into over thirty
different levels. A basically
open plan allows spaces to
compress and explode
dramatically as the heights
from floor to ceiling change
from seven to thirty feet. The
rough, ribbed texture of the
exterior walls is continued
inside, where it is played
against orange carpets and
smooth partition walls.

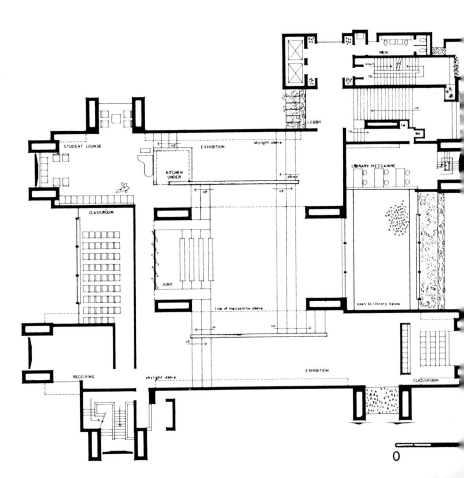

0

8

Crawford Manor Housing for the Elderly
North Frontage Road and
Park Street

architect: Paul Rudolph

This 15-story residential tower
lends quality to the growing
quantity of high-rise buildings
appearing between the Yale
campus and the Oak Street
Connector. It is one of the
several buildings included in
the city's program to provide
housing for the elderly. An
especially designed, low-cost
building-block veneer em-
phasizes the vertical aspect of
the building. A highly frag-
mented plan and the inter-
actions of the curved protruding balconies combine to
produce an active, sculptured
façade.

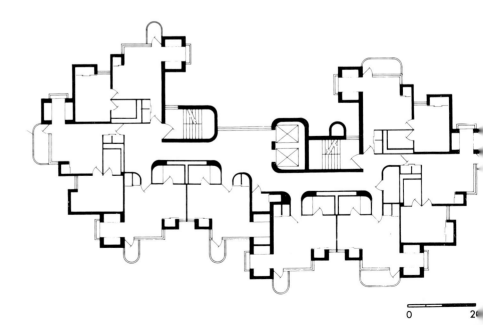

0   20

**Laboratory of Clinical
Investigation**
Howard and Davenport
Avenues

architect: Douglas Orr,
de Cossy, Winder
and Associates

Thoughtful site planning and
massing make this laboratory
tower a key component of the
growing Yale–New Haven
Medical building complex.
Laboratories and offices are
efficiently organized in a
pin-wheel plan around the
central elevator core. Hung
ceilings in the corridors
conceal the major mechanical
distribution systems servicing
each respective floor. Solid
oak doors and rough brick
walls in the corridors are
contrasted with the glass and
stainless steel technical
apparatus in the adjacent
laboratories.

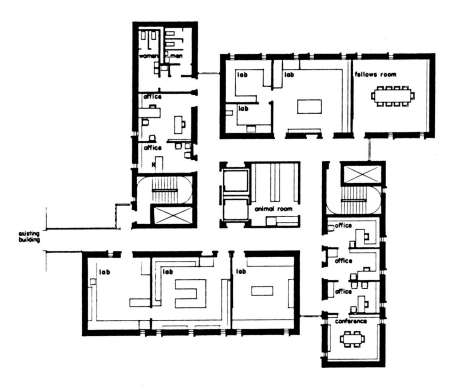

typical floor

12

**Yale Laboratory of
Epidemiology**
60 College Street

architect: Philip Johnson

Acknowledging the immense
scale of the Oak Street Connector and its frontage roads,
the Epidemiology Laboratory
responds in kind with huge
pilasters rising eight stories
from an entry-level podium.
The building's reinforced-
concrete frame is wrapped in a
tight symmetrical sandstone
and tinted glass veneer. Each
floor is individually planned
to serve the unique require-
ments established by respective laboratory needs. Narrow,
hooded windows provide a
token amount of light to the
interior while furnishing a
secondary scaling device to
the exterior elevations.

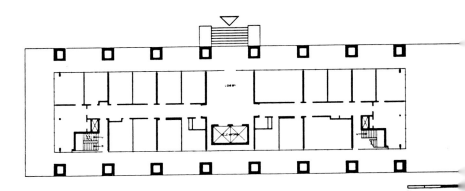

**Temple Street
Parking Garage**
Between Church and Temple
Streets at George Street

architect: Paul Rudolph

Located next to downtown
New Haven's largest depart-
ment stores, this reinforced-
concrete, self-service garage
can accommodate 1,300 cars.
Shoppers park on low-
clearance split-level ramps
and walk directly into the
adjacent stores. Stretching the
length of two full city blocks,
the garage is accessible from
cross-city streets and the
Oak Street Connector. The
curved cast-in-place railing
panels, slabs, and columns
are finished in a rugged
form-work texture.

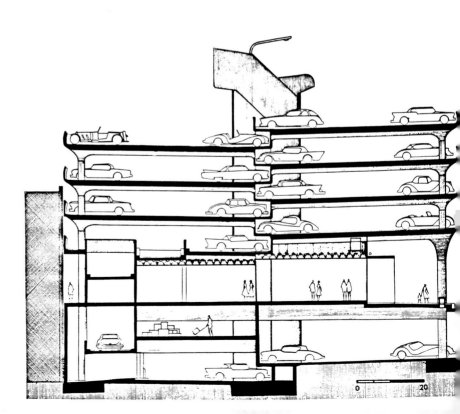

**Knights of Columbus
Headquarters Building**
1 Columbus Plaza

architect: Kevin Roche, John
Dinkeloo and Associates

Four cylindrical towers at the
corners and a central elevator
core provide support for 23
floors of office space in this
320-foot-high building. The
tile-clad towers contain stairs,
rest rooms, and mechanical
equipment. Weathering steel
girders and floor structure
span 80 feet between towers.
The glass curtain wall is held
back 5 feet for sun control
purposes. The structure is related in scale and materials
to the adjacent New Haven
Coliseum (designed by the
same architect), and the two
buildings form an awesome
landmark at the major gate-
way to the city.

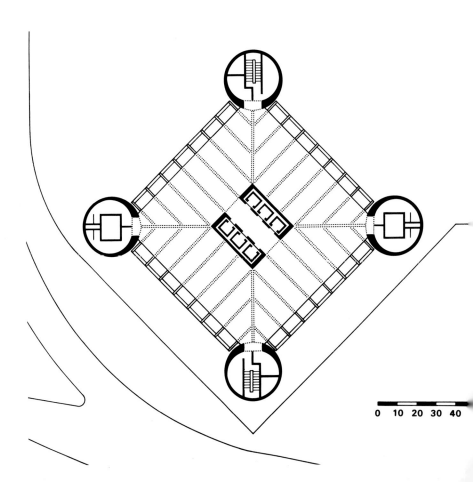

0 10 20 30 40

New Haven Coliseum
275 South Orange Street

architect: Kevin Roche, John
Dinkeloo and Associates

This immense structure covers
4½ acres on a two-block site
and consists of two basic elements: an arena with its
related facilities and a 2,400-
car, four-level parking garage
spanning the arena. The
parking garage is reached by
two double-spiral ramps
located at diagonal corners of
the complex. Stairs and ele-
vators move pedestrian traffic
to the arena concourse level
two stories above the street.
Combining the roof of the
arena with the structure of the
garage allows maximum use
of the site without impairing
pedestrian access and traffic
patterns at street level.

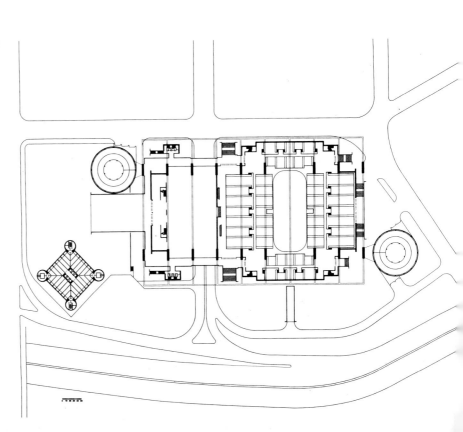

Richard C. Lee High School
100 Church Street South

architect: Kevin Roche, John
Dinkeloo and Associates

The high school is based on
the house-plan concept. Four
houses under one roof are
centered around the library.
Common facilities, such as
special-purpose classrooms,
auditorium, and cafeteria,
are on the lower level. Physical
education facilities are located
in the rear and are connected
to the main building by a
covered passage and bridge.
The building is deliberately
formal and symmetrical and is
meant to suggest both a
sense of permanence and the
seriousness and dignity of
education.

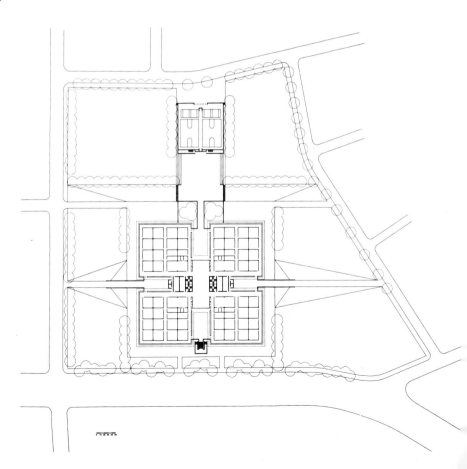

Church Street South Housing
Church Street South

architects: Charles Moore
Associates

This controversial housing
complex contains 400 units of
low-to-moderate-income
housing and 309 units of housing for the elderly. Despite
a low budget and federal
agency red tape, the project
has a strong sense of neighborhood vitality. The organiza-
tional variety of streets and
spaces and the use of bright
graphics and street landscap-
ing devices contribute to a
cohesive urban environment.
Shopping facilities, meeting
areas, and community green
spaces help define an auto-
nomous community. Perimeter
parking and pedestrian walk-
ways allow for the appropriate
segregation of people and cars.

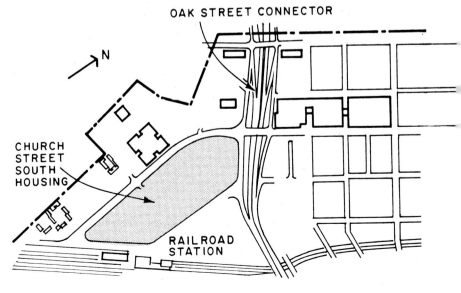

OAK STREET CONNECTOR

N

CHURCH
STREET
SOUTH
HOUSING

RAILROAD
STATION

SITE PLAN

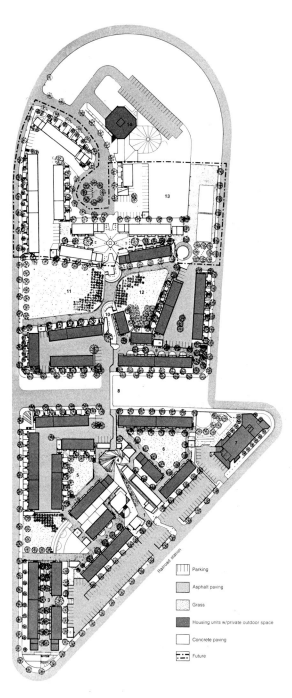

Legend

1 Entrance to pedestrian walk
2 Jose Marti Court
3 Station Court
4 Forum
1-4 Commercial space along walk
5 Christopher Green
6 Cinque Green
7 Robert T. Wolfe Public Elderly Housing
8 Columbus Ave. and location of proposed bridge
9 Malcolm Court
10 Forum
11 Great Green
12 Little Green
13 Housing not built
14 High-rise tower for elderly

Parking

Asphalt paving

Grass

Housing units w/private outdoor space

Concrete paving

Future

Central Services Building
1 State Street

architect: Douglas Orr,
de Cossy, Winder
and Associates

Previously located in separate
quarters throughout the city,
New Haven's numerous health
and welfare agencies are now
centralized in this building.
Administrative agencies
occupy the first-floor offices,
which are oriented toward the
busy downtown streets. The
consulting agencies on the
second floor face a large,
quiet, interior court. Parking
facilities are below the
building, along the periphery
of the site. Constructed of
reinforced concrete throughout, the exterior surfaces are
finished in a delicate,
vertically ribbed pattern.

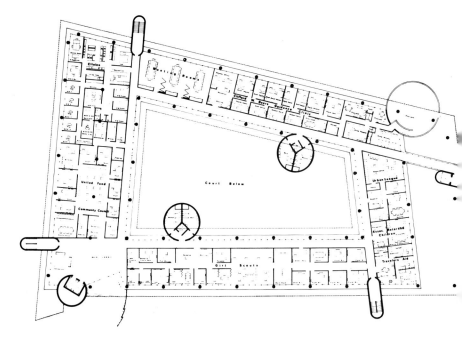

first floor p

**SAAB-SCANIA Office and
Warehouse Building**
SAAB Drive, Orange

architect: Douglas Orr,
de Cossy, Winder and
Associates

Sited on a wooden lot adjacent
to the Connecticut Turnpike,
this 100,000-square-foot building was designed to project
a bold visual impact to high-
speed traffic while maintaining
some sense of human scale
when approached by visitors.
Typical factory-building
components are used effi-
ciently to express the
sculptural forms of the west
elevation, which serves as
both the point of entry and a
billboard for the corporate
logo.

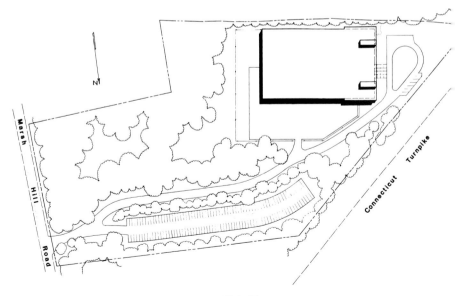

Plot Plan
SCALE: 0' 25' 50'

Standard Paint Store
500 Post Road, Orange

architect: James Terrell with
The Environmental Design
Group

Exposed bar joists and mechanical systems, cut-out
partitions, and level changes
provide an active environment within the walls of this
remodeled commercial building
located in the midst of a
sprawling Route One business
strip. The proprietor can
maintain visual control from
a cashier's cube in the center
of the store. Paint and wall-
paper displays combined with
graphic devices and large
geometrical color chips be-
come self-advertising. In-
candescent, fluorescent, and
natural light sources allow
the customer to see a color in
its intended atmosphere.

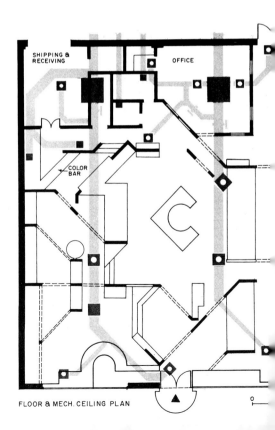

FLOOR & MECH. CEILING PLAN

Community Health Care Center
150 Sargent Drive

architect: Office of Bruce
Porter Arneill, A.I.A.

The Community Health Care
Center provides comprehensive health care services
to 40,000 people annually. The
50,000-square-foot masonry
and steel building has the
majority of its medical services
on the first floor, with administrative and secondary
services above. Patients'
waiting areas planned around
a central courtyard minimize
traffic flow to the surrounding
consultation and examination
rooms. A steel-trussed translucent entrance canopy, judi-
cious use of stairwells, and a
variety of window sizes combine to overcome the limita-
tions of the basic rectangular
form and a low budget.

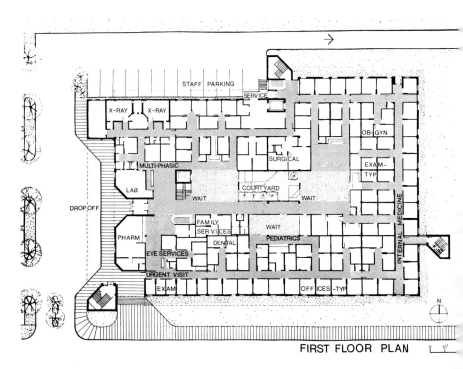

FIRST FLOOR PLAN

Fire Headquarters
952 Grand Avenue

architect: Earl Carlin
design associate: Peter Millard
associate: Paul Pozzi

A compelling structure in its own right, the New Haven Fire Headquarters is especially significant as an effective protest against the traditional dullness of municipal architecture. Four corner towers, responding to the adjacent streets, accentuate the building's angular dynamics. The exterior surfaces are patterned with varying rhythms of vertical grooves. Inside, all structural elements and mechanical apparatus are exposed. The functional integrity of the plan is reinforced by the use of simple and maintenance-free materials throughout the building.

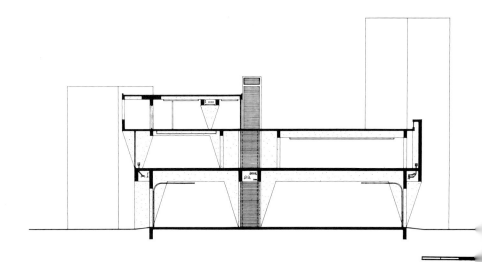

0

Wooster Square

The Wooster Square area qualified in 1950 as one of the city's most deteriorated communities. Encouraged by the 1954 housing act, the City Redevelopment office and the ad hoc Wooster Square Renewal Committee established a comprehensive program for rehabilitating the neighborhood. The Conte School, Columbus Mall, Court Street, and Greene Street Housing became the vanguard projects, while hundreds of community-motivated citizens undertook to repair their properties at their own expense. The result is a planned community within the city and the reestablishment of a definitive neighborhood.

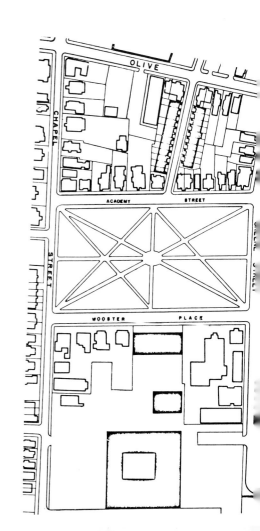

Towne House on the Park
Green Street and Hughes
Place

architects: Office of William
Mileto

This project contains 36 units
of one- and two-bedroom
apartments. The one-bedroom
units are located a half level
below grade, with the two-story,
two-bedroom units above. A
large enclosed court, removed
from street traffic and noise,
provides a play area for
children. Tenant parking
facilities occur to the north of
the court. Concrete-block
bearing walls and wood joists
form the basis of the structural
system. Exterior walls, painted
an off-white, are punctuated
by redwood trim around
windows and doors.

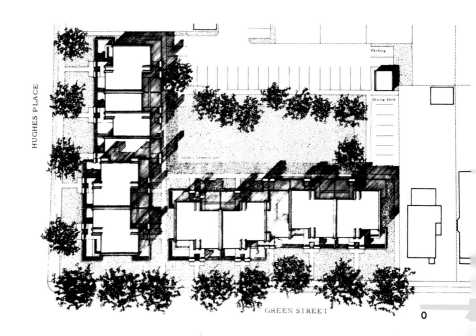

**Matthew Ruoppolo Manor
Housing for the Elderly**
470–480 Ferry Street

architects: Gilbert Switzer and
Associates

One of Connecticut's first HUD
Turnkey efforts, this 16-unit
project makes optimum use of
a cramped site while relating
inoffensively to its wood-frame,
residential neighborhood.
Community spaces inside the
building open onto the entry
court and recreation garden.
The Y-shaped plan with a
central service core eliminates
the need for the long, dreary
corridors typical of public
housing. Elevator lobbies with
large windows are brightly
furnished to encourage social-
izing, and most apartments
have private balconies or
terraces.

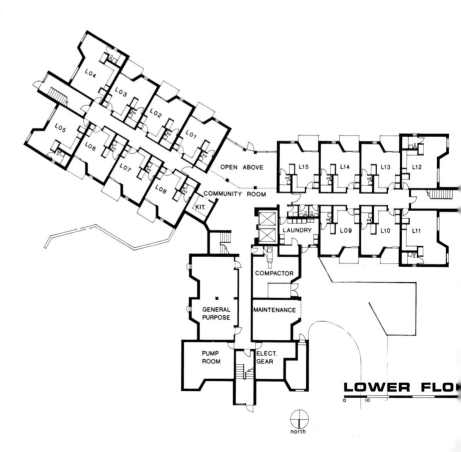

LOWER FLO

north

Chermayeff Residence
28 Lincoln Street

architect: Serge Chermayeff

This one-story house is zoned to
provide maximum privacy and
quiet. Designed as a variation
of the architect's comprehen-
sively developed proposals
for medium-density, cluster
prototypes, the house
performs admirably as an
isolated unit on a traditional,
residential street. The
programmatic needs of three
distinct domains with
appropriate buffer zones
between are logically reflected
in the plan. A series of walled
courts becomes in fair
weather a private extension
of interior spaces.

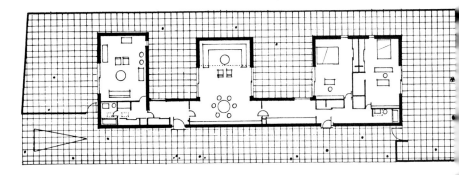

0

42

**Yale University Health
Services Building**
17 Hillhouse Avenue

architects: Westermann-Miller
Associates

Located at the center of the
campus, this six-story lime-
stone and glass building serves
the medical needs of the
30,000 people who make up
the Yale community. Orga-
nized as an affiliate of the
Grace-New Haven Hospital,
the building provides a wide
range of diagnostic and
treatment facilities for non-
acute health services as a
part of a unique prepaid medical health program. A 70-bed
infirmary on the fourth and fifth
floors can be doubled in case
of an epidemic, while a non-
appointment clinic for out-
patient service is available at
entry level.

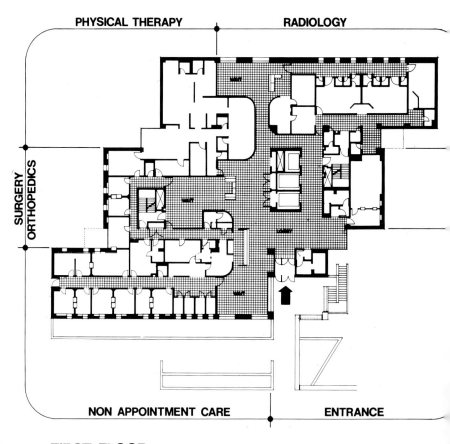

PHYSICAL THERAPY   RADIOLOGY

SURGERY
ORTHOPEDICS

NON APPOINTMENT CARE   ENTRANCE

FIRST FLOOR

**Becton Engineering and
Applied Science Center**
3 Hillhouse Avenue

architect: Marcel Breuer

Built only a few feet from the
curb, the Becton Laboratory
looms massively above Hillhouse Avenue. Six huge concrete columns punctuate an
arcade that runs the length of
the building at entry level.
Uniform grids of precast-concrete panels form the front
and rear façades. A depart-
mental library, classrooms,
and labs take up the first five
floors, with mechanicals on
the top floor. Beneath a plaza
at the rear of the building
is a 275-seat auditorium. Tun-
nels connect the structure
with two adjacent intradepart-
mental laboratory buildings.

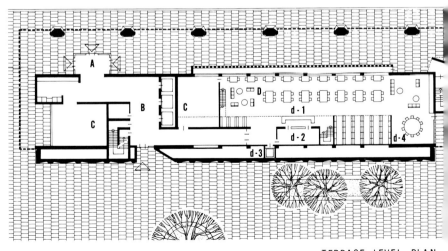

TERRACE LEVEL PLAN

0 10 20 30 40 50   FEET

Beinecke Rare Books Library
Wall and High Streets

architect: Gordon Bunshaft of
Skidmore, Owings and Merrill

Translucent marble panels
admit a warm light to the
interior of the boxlike
structure that serves as an
exhibition area and entry point
for this largely subterranean
building. Books and manu-
scripts are stored in a series
of climatically controlled
stacks. Administrative facilities
below ground open to a
sunken sculpture court
exhibiting a marble landscape
by Noguchi. A paved plaza
becomes an effective transi-
tional device between this
imposing structure and its
neoclassic and neo-Gothic
neighbors.

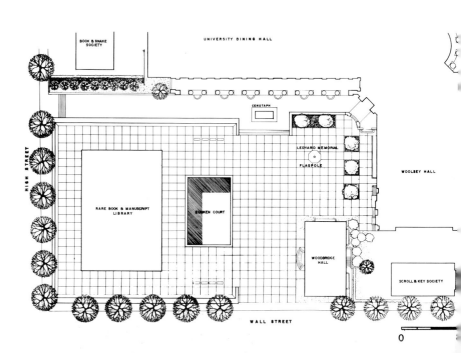

0

Yale Computer Center
60 Sachem Street

architect: Gordon Bunshaft
of Skidmore, Owings and
Merrill

Located diagonally across
Prospect Street from the
David S. Ingalls Rink, the
Computer Center is a classic
example of the Skidmore,
Owings and Merrill idiom. Its
tinted glass and steel
elevations relate inoffensively
to the varied architectural
heritage of the adjacent
buildings. Its precise detailing
and machinelike quality are
particularly appropriate to the
computer technology it serves.

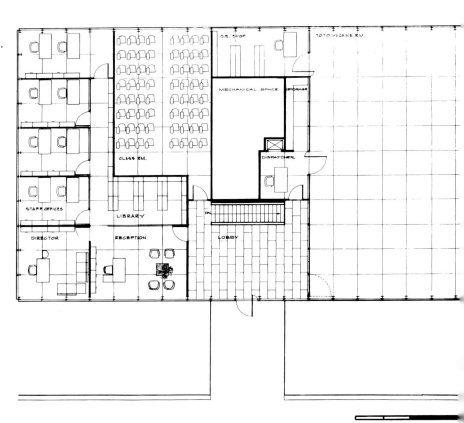

0

David S. Ingalls Rink
73 Sachem Street

architect: Eero Saarinen

A reinforced-concrete arch spanning 270 feet provides the visual and structural backbone for this controversial skating rink. A system of cables hung between the arch and the low peripheral walls supports a compound-curved wood-plank deck. Exposed mechanical apparatus and the rugged, utilitarian treatment of the interior are skillfully played against the sophisticated contours of the exterior walls and roof.

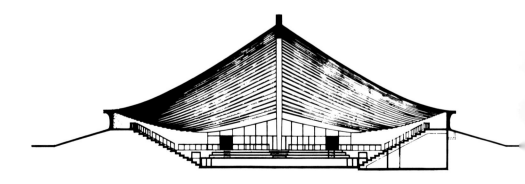

0

**Greeley Memorial Forestry
Laboratory**
370 Prospect Street

architect: Paul Rudolph

Solid precast stone walls form
a podium beneath the main
floor of this multipurpose
laboratory. Precast-concrete,
Y-shaped columns support a
flat roof that overhangs
set-back walls. Interior walls
stop short of the ceiling,
allowing natural light to the
interior spaces. A screen
suspended from the west end
of the roof provides protection
from the afternoon sun, as
well as providing a means of
visually terminating the
downhill side of the building.

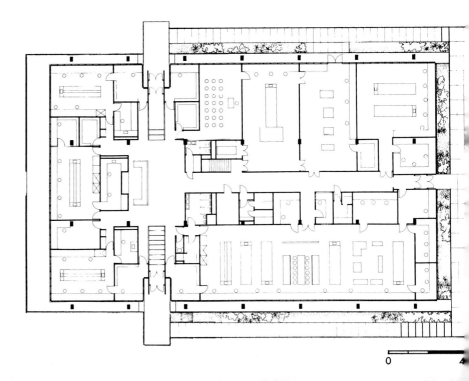

0   4

Yale Kline Biology Laboratory
Sachem Street

architect: Philip Johnson

A dramatic addition to the
New Haven skyline, the Kline
Biology Laboratory forms the
hub of the University's
burgeoning science-building
complex. Dark sandstone and
glazed brick form a smooth,
muscular skin around the
reinforced-concrete frame.
Closely spaced, rounded
pilasters accentuate the
tower's strong vertical aspect.
An underground library and
twelve stories of laboratories
are topped by a floor of dining
facilities and a three-story,
Parthenon-like mechanical loft.

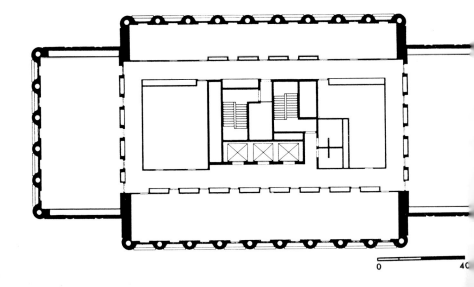

0   40

58

Nuclear Structure Laboratory
51 Sachem Street

architect: Douglas Orr,
de Cossy, Winder
and Associates

Embedded in the north end of
Yale's expanding science
complex, the truncated,
pyramidic earth forms of the
Nuclear Structure Laboratory
provide an appropriate sanctu-
ary for the unique Emperor
tandem Van de Graaff electro-
static accelerator. The precise,
versatile accelerator is 125
feet long, weighs
approximately 250 tons, and is
capable of generating up to 15
million volts. The huge vault
containing the accelerator is
adjoined by administrative
offices and laboratories for
associated research.

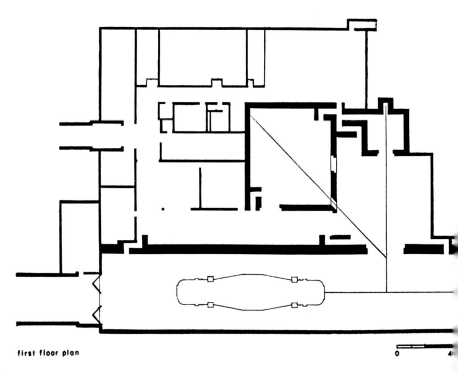

first floor plan

0   4

Yale Kline Geology Laboratory
210 Whitney Avenue

architect: Philip Johnson

A spacious, skylit stairway
connects three stories of
classrooms, laboratories, and
offices in this compact,
efficiently planned building.
Linked by a bridge to the
Peabody Museum, the
Laboratory is an effective
counterbalance to the
Museum's neo-Gothic profile.
Rounded, protruding vertical
forms establish a regular bay
system along the glazed brick
and dark sandstone façades.
Because of the need for
consistent, controlled light in
the laboratories, fenestration
is relatively minimal except
for the offices on the north
side.

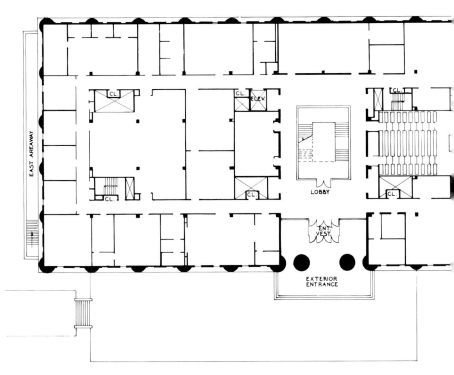

Whitney Avenue Fire Station
352 Whitney Avenue

architect: Earl Carlin
design associate: Peter Millard
associate: Paul Pozzi

Situated on a broad street in a
primarily residential area, the
Whitney Avenue Fire Station is
appropriately scaled to its
environment. The dark brick
and clapboard-formed
concrete exterior is activated
by stairways and light wells
extending from a basically
rectangular plan. Precast T
beams span between concrete
columns within the sidewalls.
The effectively planned fire-
men's quarters on the second
floor reflect a consideration for
functional design that is
apparent throughout the
building.

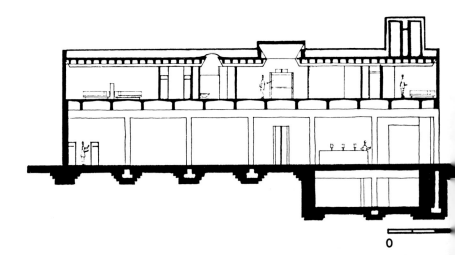

0

Mitarachi Residence
120 Deepwood Drive, Hamden

architect: Paul Mitarachi

This house was designed to take full advantage of a southern exposure and a dramatic view of New Haven. Because of the sloping site, the house was split into four levels in a basically open plan. All spaces, except for the bedrooms, are oriented southward toward privacy and the view. Circulation space for the entire house is efficiently provided by the stairway and its landings. Laminated wood beams and stud walls are protected for the weather by vertical, tongue-and-groove, Philippine mahogany sheathing.

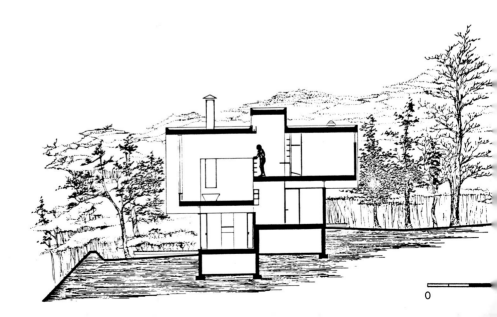

0

Northern Branch YMCA
1605 Sherman Avenue,
Hamden

architects: Harold Roth –
Edward Saad

Built as the first part of a three-phase program, this structure has a swimming pool and a number of other recreational facilities. A central skylighted hall eases traffic circulation and serves as a common point of entry to the various adjacent facilities. Coffered-concrete floor systems span between brick-bearing walls. Maintenance-free materials throughout, including quarry tile, carpet, and laminated maple, add to the building's attractiveness and durability. Future expansion will include a gymnasium, handball and squash courts, and additional social activity rooms.

FUTURE EXPANSION

FEET 50 100 200

NORTH

Ridge Hill School
120 Carew Road, Hamden

architects: Harold Roth –
Edward Saad

Organized around a team-
teaching program using four
large learning center areas,
the Ridge Hill School enrolls
650 elementary school students
in an ungraded curriculum.
Efficient interior circulation is
achieved via a central skylighted rampway connecting
the various levels necessitated
by a gently sloping site.
Vehicular and pedestrian traffic are appropriately segre-
gated, and school bus loading
occurs under cover at the
lower level. In anticipation of
evening and summer use,
the plan allows for ready access to community-oriented
facilities without disruption of
academic areas.

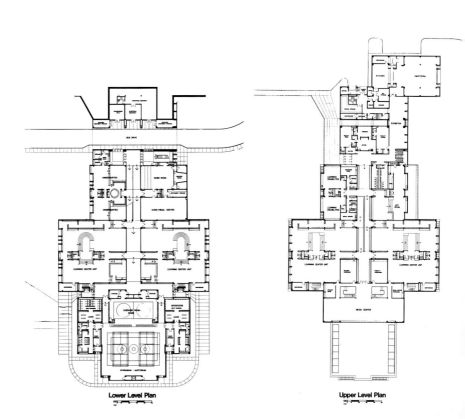

Lower Level Plan

Upper Level Plan

**Samuel Morse and Ezra Stiles
Residential Colleges**
Broadway and Tower Parkway

architect: Eero Saarinen and
Associates

The first addition to Yale's
residential college system
since the 1930's, Morse and
Stiles demonstrate a
calculated respect for their
neo-Gothic neighbors.
Gateways, walks, and
courtyards establish an
effective sequence of spaces
between and around the
colleges. Ranging in heights
from one to thirteen stories,
each component of the plan
maintains a consistent scale.
The carefully integrated
sculpture of Constantine
Nivola accentuates the
project's compelling
geometric quality. This quality
is continued inside, where
polygonal floor plans create
a wide variety of residential
units.

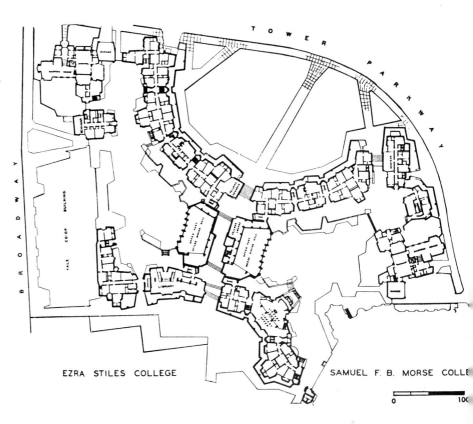

EZRA STILES COLLEGE

SAMUEL F. B. MORSE COLLE

**Dwight Cooperative
Town Houses**
99 Edgewood Avenue

architects: Gilbert Switzer and
Associates

The Dwight Coop is an 80-unit
town house complex providing
a wide range of apartment
sizes for low- and moderate-
income families. The com-
mendable site plan segregates
vehicular and pedestrian
traffic and shows potential for
versatile development of the
interior courtyards. A circular
spray pool, playground area,
and renovated brick carriage
house add to a sense of
community, while individual
patios and a direct circulation plan allow some degree
of privacy.

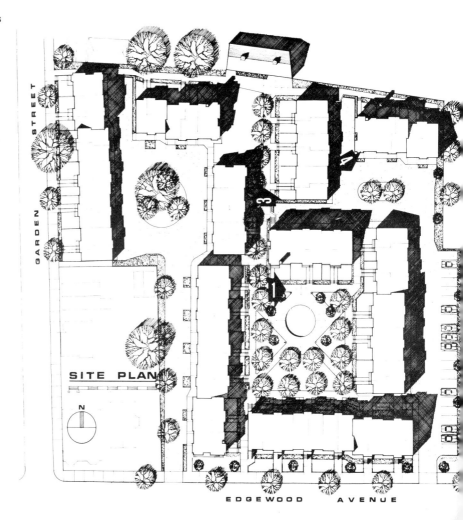

SITE PLAN

N

**Mount Zion Seventh-Day
Adventist Church**
64 Marlboro Street, Hamden

architect: Earl Carlin
design associate: Peter Millard
associate: Paul Pozzi

The architectural potential
of simple forms and materials
is effectively exploited in this
low-budget community church.
Pews for a congregation of
350 face a chancel that
includes the speaker's rostrum,
space for a choir of 30, and
the baptistry. Custom-made
concrete blocks and the
fragmentation of exterior
volumes significantly reduce
the scale of the church to that
of its immediate residential
environment. The strong,
simple quality of each elevation
emphasizes the simplicity of
the liturgy within.

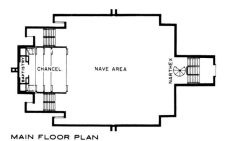

MAIN FLOOR PLAN

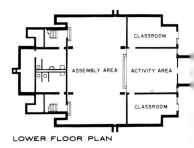

LOWER FLOOR PLAN

0

**West Rock Nature-
Recreation Center**
Wintergreen Avenue

architects: Harold Roth –
Edward Saad

The use of dramatic wood
trusses above a system of
exposed cedar post, beam, and
plank construction gives this
small public nature center an
informal, rugged appeal.
The building is situated along
the entrance walkway to the
nature-center grounds near oc-
casional animal shelters. It
is used for orientation talks,
displays, movies, and related
conferences. A staff of three
naturalists shares work areas
in balcony alcoves above the
quarry-tiled exhibit area.

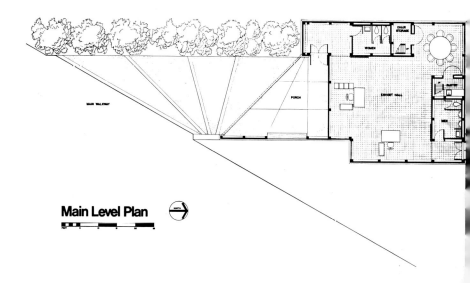

Main Level Plan

Oriental Masonic Gardens
50 Wilmot Road

architect: Paul Rudolph

This low- and moderate-income housing project was assembled with factory-built units stacked together in two-story cruciform configurations. Twelvefoot-wide modules accommodate two- through five-bedroom apartments with living-dining-kitchen areas on the lower floor. The lower and upper floors are at ninety degrees to each other and define two sides of a private courtyard. The plywood modules, with built-in mechanical and structural systems, were assembled in Maryland and trucked to New Haven, where they were craned into place and bolted together.

Gay Residence
13 Tulip Tree Lane,
Woodbridge

designer: Don Metz

A central stair system connects
four levels of living space,
providing varying degrees of
privacy in this multizoned
home. Inset clerestory glazing,
skylights, and window areas
make maximum use of the
southern exposure and admit
direct sunlight most of the
day. Built-in furniture, integral
with the architecture, occurs
throughout the house. Interior
finishes include imported tile,
red oak floors and woodwork,
and white gypsum walls and
ceilings. Exterior siding is
bleached, quarter-grain fir.

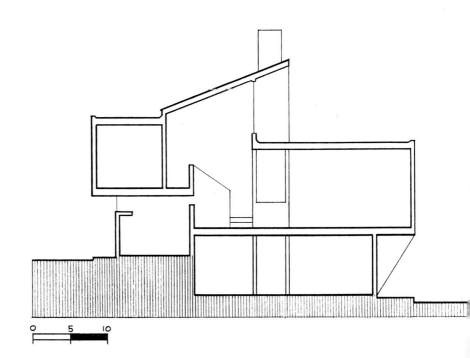

0   5   10

84

**St. John Vianney
Parish Complex**
Palace and Grove Streets,
West Haven

architects: Kosinski Associates

The two interior courts act as
buffer zones between church,
rectory, and social hall in
this parish complex. The three
distinct parts are linked by a
covered brick arcade, which
opens onto a landscaped
area adjacent to a parking lot
for 200 cars. Philosophical
and financial considerations
called for a design stressing
simplicity and dignity rather
than the forms of the traditional
monumental temple. In the
church wing there is a sparing
use of form and materials.
Light wells located above the
liturgical symbols add to the
atmosphere of the religious
celebrations.

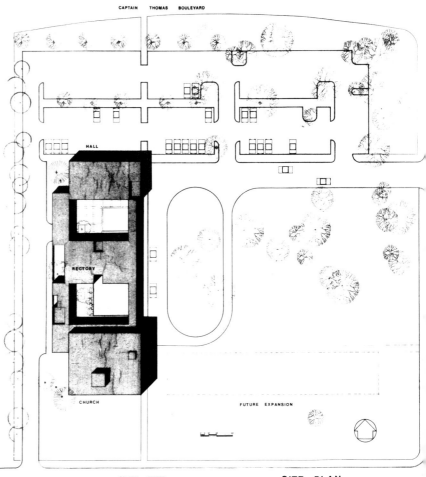

SITE PLAN

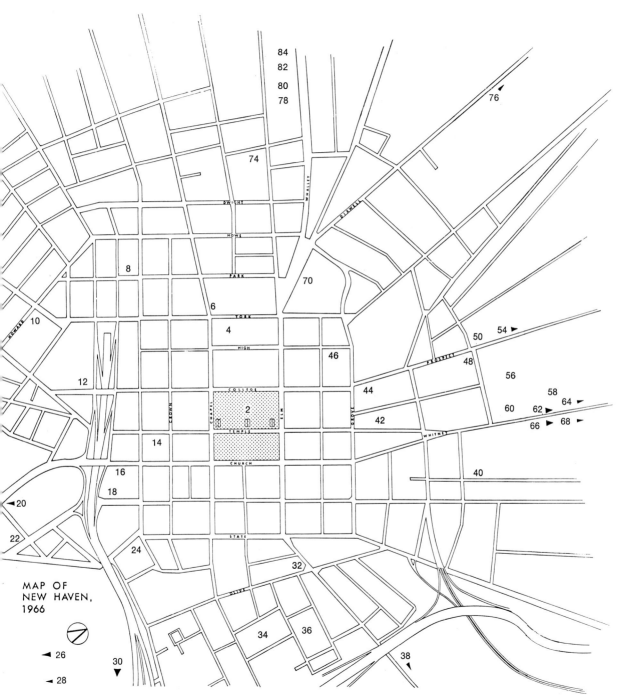

MAP OF
NEW HAVEN,
1966

Introduction	Yuji Noga
New Haven Common	Yuji Noga
Yale Art Gallery	Yuji Noga
Yale School of Art and Architecture	Yuji Noga
Crawford Manor Housing for the Elderly	Yuji Noga
Laboratory of Clinical Investigation	Yuji Noga
Yale Laboratory of Epidemiology	Yuji Noga
Temple Street Parking Garage	Yuji Noga
Knights of Columbus Headquarters Building	Chalmer Alexander
New Haven Coliseum	Chalmer Alexander
Richard C. Lee High School	Ezra Stoller © ESTO
Church Street South Housing	Lee Ryder, A. Wade Perry
Central Services Building	Ezra Stoller © ESTO
SAAB-SCANIA Office and Warehouse Building	Ezra Stoller © ESTO
Standard Paint Store	Robert Perron
Community Health Care Center	Bill Maris
Fire Headquarters	Yuji Noga
Wooster Square	Yuji Noga
Towne House on the Park	Yuji Noga
Matthew Ruoppolo Manor Housing for the Elderly	Thomas A. Brown
Chermayeff Residence	Norman McGrath
Yale University Health Services Building	Bill Rothschild
Becton Engineering and Applied Science Center	Susan Willy
Beinecke Rare Books Library	Yuji Noga
Yale Computer Center	Yuji Noga
David S. Ingalls Rink	Yuji Noga
Greeley Memorial Forestry Laboratory	Yuji Noga
Yale Kline Biology Laboratory	Yuji Noga
Nuclear Structure Laboratory	Yuji Noga
Yale Kline Geology Laboratory	Yuji Noga
Whitney Avenue Fire Station	Yuji Noga
Mitarachi Residence	Yuji Noga
Northern Branch YMCA	Robert Perron
Ridge Hill School	Robert Perron
Samuel Morse and Ezra Stiles Residential Colleges	Yuji Noga
Dwight Cooperative Town Houses	Thomas A. Brown
Mount Zion Seventh-Day Adventist Church	Yuji Noga
West Rock Nature-Recreation Center	Robert Perron
Oriental Masonic Gardens	Donald Luckenbill
Gay Residence	Susan Willy
St. John Vianney Parish Complex	McLeod

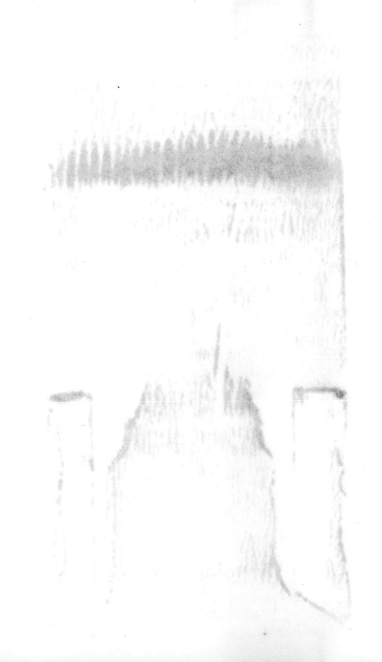

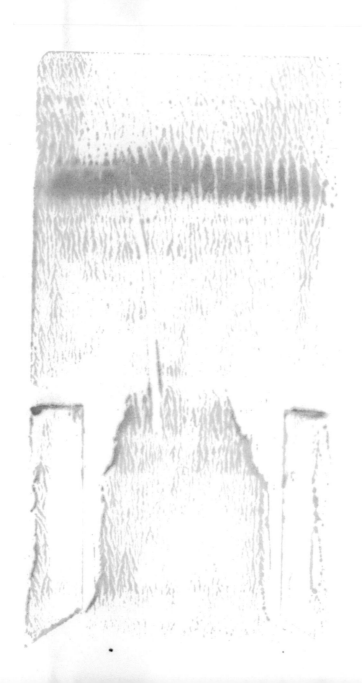